poems.

too small to read.

JEREMY M. DOWNES

Library of Congress Control Number: 2012941893

ISBN 9780985770303

Downes, Jeremy M.
Poems. Too Small to Read.

Published by Summerfield Publishing,
New Plains Press
P.O. Box 1946
Auburn, AL 36831-1946
Newplainspress.com

Composition and cover design by Emily Wilkins

ACKNOWLEDGMENTS

"The Bicycle Accident," *SPSM&H* #20 (1992).
"The Book of Lot," Third Prize, Murphy Memorial Award, NFSPS Contest 2007. *Encore: 2007 Prize Poem Anthology.*
"Bottle the Sun," Third Prize, Dr. Zylpha Mapp Robinson International Poetry Award 2010. *Möbius, the Poetry Magazine*, January 2011.
"Flight," First Prize, Donald D. Dungey Memorial Award, NFSPS Contest 1998. *Encore: 1998 Prize Poem Anthology.*
"The gecko with her name across its tail," *Möbius, the Poetry Magazine* (2008).
"Kia Writes the Microwaves," Third Prize, Arizona State Poetry Society Award, NFSPS Contest 2006. *Encore: 2006 Prize Poem Anthology.*
"Kudzu Harp," *Möbius, the Poetry Magazine* (2008).
"The Muse at Tsavo," *Möbius, the Poetry Magazine* (2008)
"Rabbit Watches," Third Prize, Morton D. Prouty, Jr., Memorial Award, NFSPS Contest 1999. *Encore: 1999 Prize Poem Anthology.*
"Sirens," Second Prize, New York Poetry Forum Award, NFSPS Contest 2006. *Encore: 2006 Prize Poem Anthology.*
"Vilas Zoo in Winter," Third Prize, Prouty Memorial Award, NFSPS Contest 2007. *Encore: 2007 Prize Poem Anthology.*
"The Woman Who Borrowed the Sun," Third Prize, Nebraska State Poetry Society Award, NFSPS Contest 2007. *Encore: 2007 Prize Poem Anthology.*

In addition, grateful acknowledgment is made to New Dawn Unlimited Press and the Alabama State Poetry Society, which published several of these poems in Dark Village Haiku, *the winner of the 2007 Morris Memorial Chapbook Award.*

for Alan & Claire

CONTENTS

poems.

too small to read.

Too Small to Read

She holds it stuck, like stamp or crumb,
on one tender finger.

Her eyes are vague puzzles, vague distaste.

"Too small to read," she says,
and her tongue

licks my warm poem away.

If only your smile
were not clouds

in this swift river of glass.

FLIGHT

Earlier today I taught
our toddler how to make a paper
airplane, folding the blank sheets in long white
lines, into triangles of space; I told him there
were other ways, for I remembered slicing air
in loops, overs and unders, but I'd quite
forgotten those. Ours flew its caper
inside and quickly caught

somewhere behind the shelf,
so we folded a dozen more,
filling our small rooms with papery flight
thoughtless of consequence, much less picking the lost
constructions up from the carpet (and the high cost
correction bears, getting all set right
of all that's gone misdone before:
—cleaning up for yourself).

At times, play makes the clay
seem almost real. Breathing the life
from one generation into the next
is partly what words do, but don't our actions also
(moreso?) shape these childhoods? I plan planes made of balsa
for another day, and feel the effects
of children on fathers. My wife
stops in wonder—what to say?—

coming from work back home
to find her house in flight; the day's
delight of crashes, curves, and spins returning
to the supper table; and all the housework left
undone. She smiles patiently, but she's been bereft
of airy voyaging. So we keep learning
'til late, folding wings in new ways,
flying our bright sky's dome.

KIA WRITES THE MICROWAVES

Kia writes the microwaves
        sizzling yesterday's browned grief;
Kia reads the manuals, finds
        the pounds per square inch pressure
        shrugged in the can-opener's blade.

Kia writes the spray and *whuush*
        of dishwashers striking up at dawn;
Kia watches as the maple knifeblock does its work;
        as the salad-spinner spins;
        as the blender threshes, combs, combines.

Kia writes refrigerated lyrics, the buzzing light's
        fluorescent prose, and Kia wants and
Kia wants to chant the epic of laminate floors,
        script the toaster's pulp fiction,
        sing the kitchen's effable romance.

BALLADE: FEVER

The world kaleidoscopes to this
small nursery, braided with sun
through the blinds, and the gurgling hiss
the vaporizer makes. My son
coughs the desperate rasp of one
undone by weariness, and fever
shines its candleflame through his shiver
and his sweat. His mother stands
him up in midair, as if to deliver
this child, like a fire, in my hands.

I feel the heat before I kiss
the blazing flesh, feel the just-spun
thread of a life begin to crisp
into something else. What's begun
can always have an end—what's done
began somewhere. And now, if ever,
I hate the stoic philosophers
for teaching me the cautious stance,
the dispassionate will to sever
this child (like a fire in my hands)

from myself. So all raw fear is
shorn away. I pace from the sun
to the shadow and back with this
lightening burden of fire, and run
from Southwell's burning babe to Donne,
to Jonson, Thomas, Plath, as ever
in search of a right rasped word, lever
of language, and love where it stands,
and hate that love and fear deliver
this childlike fire into my hands.

The child burns, my words are a river
aflame in language's constant shiver—
and we've tried everything we can.
I breathe my poems to this fever,
this child, like a fire, in my hands.

THE POEM THEY LOVE

This is the poem they love,
       for it includes a train,
       slowly pulling in
       to a dark village,

and the words line up like blocks
       two of each kind
       together, holding hands, even
       as dark clouds burn lower, and lower.

LOVE LYRIC

my Styro-
foam

poem

BOTTLE THE SUN

The buildings do their best to hold it in,
dark brick facades absorbing old Sol's glance.

Surely the kindly sun will help us now.
Our little photovoltaics charge and glimmer

glamorous in the light. Arched porticos
bake us with radiant heat. The AC roars.

We have lived too long, and the blues guitar
mumbling from the quadrangle agrees:

hard rains gonna fall; hard rains gonna fall.

We have lived too long and slept too late,
and we have eaten and drunk too much.

My labmate drinks a beaker of the old south,
barrel-aged nepenthe, hipflask Hippocrene,

says it's all a hoax. The ice-shelf shifts in the heart—
the algae blooms—our students' Hummers, Cayennes,

imitation Cobras and Corvettes—these wait for us.
We have driven too far, too fast, too drunk.

the sun keeps shining through the pouring rain

And yet the parking deck pours oily wash,
steaming from the sun, into the weedy concrete slab

that forty years ago was Muscadine Creek,
fringed with wild grape and wild honeysuckle,

a neck of woodland fresh for sparking, spooning.
I turn back to the gas chromatograph,

bottle my response, listen for the ionizing flame,
torching still more of this small flask of sun.

NOAH'S WIFE

The tigers have parted,
the goats stay where they are;
the gazelles will linger,
the sparrows crack their grain,
and the air its bloom entice.

Pretty bows, wrappings—
yet I cannot trust the way the shuttling
of the moon weaves daily heaven's web,
nor that the kindling sky believes
nor that the kindling cedar roof denies:

Our firmament's a broken bowl
scarred with wishing, with washing, with use,
its color dulled against
those deep fresh cracks of shattering.

THE WOMAN WHO BORROWED THE SUN

Rain again, days of it, light bulbs flickering like bent leaves
and the morning thunderstorm boring in.

The sandbox pools six inches of red water;
the wheelbarrow sloshes its fullness;
the power goes.

I am not causing this; my anxieties, my bleakness, my solitude
were worth a rainy day or two.

But not even your ocean flight, our child's, makes me this weepy;
I have to wring the roses out
before I let them in the house.

The rain-gauge is under water; tall ships go by on the fjord
that just last week was our back yard. I had to let the ducks inside.

The house without your laughter is a water-heavy sponge—green, I
    think,
aching with shingle grit and the weight of resolute airplanes,

and our heavy house slides on its slab foundation
down the hill atop the runoff Alabama mud.

Trains stop sixty miles away to let their passengers canoe
between the branches of live oak, cell-phone towers, clouds.
I sometimes thought—

before our new blue SUV washed down the hill, shiny tail lights
glittering above the flood—that I could drive my way out
of this sinkhole.

But I thought too that it's my fault, that it would follow me,
hollow ground falling beneath the fat black tires.
This rain's too big for the both of us.

Come home. I'll finish this note now, tuck it in a warmer, drier place—
the bottle of wedding wine we've saved—and float it off to you.
It's getting worse, this rain. I think I'll climb in, too.

Desire will not end
the way you expect,

                    buckled
into your body.

THE BICYCLE ACCIDENT

Unthinkingly, I remember your glove, blood
caked in it, that I washed out in the sink
the best I could; you were out of the hospital,
lying in the unmade bed that that apartment
flaunted hugely. I had said that your face was too good
to be real — that scars would help, and made you drink
chicken soup from a mug; you calmed and slept.
And calm your clothes soaked in cool water, the way
my mother taught me. The stains I could deal with,
but not the asphalt's jagged tears. Now, I think,
I couldn't even do that; my mind like white porcelain
is full of your face and the blood of your glove.

THE PILLOW BOOK (HAPPY POEM #4)

Reading Sei Shonagon's lists of things, even her list of *hateful things,*
even her list of *things that give an icky feeling*
even her list of *things that I made up:*

it's not the lists themselves, though item after item shine.
It's not *a mantis broken in the sash.*
It's not *the crack in one's Chinese mirror from Cho-fu-sa;*

rather, it is that feel of a mind so arranging itself that images,
like tools—*the brush, the silver tweezers, the cherry-pruning saw*
—should slip just so into appointed places

as though all the untowardness of a normal life
were tallied up at one's pillow and not—
not quite, not always—found wanting

Thirteen Cormorants

1.
Between thirty whitecaps frothing,
the rain sizzling in, wind and water twisting,
one cormorant holds still.

2.
The cormorant's hooked bill spits the yellowjack,
like a mind too set in its course.

3.
Male and female created he them:
Kwer-kwer, they grunt like small pigs in the nest.

4.
The world, the woman, the word—they all mean the same thing.
The cormorant combs the waves,
lost in one thing.

5.
I don't know *what* I want. The pontoon
awash with waves is not the waves' home.
The cormorant points north, swart form in a coarse wind.

6.
Sun batters the deck; sun shatters the sealight, and
the green boat creaks in the heat. A cormorant dives,
and in that gray-green dark it thrives.

7.
Now how do you like your romance?
she says. Outside dance the cormorants;
Over easy, I mumble in answer.

8.
Every day, over again, the sea weaves
almost the same pattern of arching waves
along the pier. A lone cormorant
lets me know that it's a curse, this many wives.

9.
Disaster plasters us with salt and grit, masters us all.
You can blame anyone you want: it triangulates,
like a cormorant's webbed foot.

10.
A scarred bus rolls down to the beach;
the people yell, waving their iron, each
spiked urchin armed, anchored out of reach.
The cormorant arcs onward, black letter
on a deep gray field.

11.
The cormorant's discourse is silence, as after a divorce
the oftenest option is silence, your intercourse
interrupted by black shadows, the tide lunging back to enforce
with all its memories the things that you thought might float.

12.
How long can one summer linger?
Ask the beach people, the dark bodies who finger
the thin gray sand alone, and drink. The black birds
buckle away in mid-flight from the stones, the words.

13.
All afternoon it has rained, hard, like the particle
theory cresting the wave in a *Nature* article
you read in another life. The cormorant sits its stained perch,
its eyes out there diving, fishing. And so, too, you search.

Fear

She wants the biggest dog she can find, a
        Russian Wolfhound or a Newfoundland
to walk her rumbling past
        her own new-published books,
bright and hideously familiar
        inside the bookstore window.

Tonight she'll dance and twist beside a
        heavy metal speaker, feeling thunder
tremble in her thighs from its sheer noise;
        she thinks her children won't grow old
if she and the world just stay awake.

        But just now she luxuriates atop a
trembling aluminum ladder, two fingers hung
        on a leafthick gutter, three fathoms
over the flagstone; it is in moments
        of giddy joy like this
she fears her husband will die young.

And both at once (Happy Poem #3)

. . . and be happy the way your terrycloth bathrobe knows
its happiness, cozy with night and flannel pajamas, reading mystery
under a pool of eager light

. . . and be happy the way your terrycloth bathrobe knows
its wicked happiness after a shower, tugging gently each warm drop
from your body flowing like water

Vilas Zoo in Winter

Jill is at the zoo, her blue eyes
are at the zoo, she pulls her coat close
in the blue wind.

Shit steams in the yards; the animals
are shaggy with cold, and again the lion
protests the daylight.

Ice ices the walks, the kind
that brittly cracks white and small
and maybe melts

under Jill's white sneakers. She sees
the cold otter chasing a curled oakleaf,
bunching and thrusting

as an otter does. The seamless world
is rubbled and split in the repeating roar
that the lion roars.

AND AFTER THUNDER THE ENDLESS RAIN

Tonight you dream the old Homeric dream,
again, where you race the endless cycling plain:
Escaping, chasing, who there will tell you?
In these dreams they are one and the same.

You run. A burning begins in your lungs
and lunges in your throat and takes your tongue:
You pant like a dog. Like brittle tin or greasy lead
your iron knees crumble beneath you, numbed.

(It was the meeting that failed you. The stoplight
someone ran. The noiseless dark of the house.
The weight of your inexorable addiction. The things
your body does. Or what your brother told you.)

Sometimes in days of stained aluminum rain it seems
almost a less frightening dream among the dreams.

A SORROW OF OGRES

1.

Where the sadness comes in
is that the real work lies elsewhere and in
the duration of the cello's second note and after
in the dilemma of blue in thick acrylic,
especially through time and sun.

2.

Tomatoes sadden me, the gel of their mirroring viscera,
like eyes, but with seeds,
and their ineluctable red frames as strong as houses,
and what saddens me most is architecture's sheer futility,
like a blood blister

beckoning everyone to dig, dig, deeper dig,
and root the simulacra out.

3.

I am darkened by old men whose wristwatches grow loose
around their lightening bones so gradually they only notice as they slip
and then forget.

*   *   *

Under the tree these three agree that children
Are most frightening, most terrible of all.

RE: FWD: FINAL ASSIGNMENT: WRITE A POEM USING YAMS AND FROGS

Hi Professor!

This was a hard assignment! Even when I baked the yams for
      an hour and a half, and mashed them up (and added
      a little butter!), it wasn't as though I could

write with them. It turned out more like finger painting, but
      really thick. I know you said to email, so
      I borrowed my roommate's camera and I'm attaching a
      .jpeg;

I hope that works. Let me know if you have trouble opening it.
      At first I tried to write with the raw yams, peeled
      and not peeled, but it was chalky and pasty—

even harder to read than the mashed yams. The frogs were hard
      to catch, but I did get some. My roommate
      works in a pet store, so she knows a lot about frogs, but

she's visiting her folks this weekend. I wish she'd been here,
      'cause she helped a lot with your assignment
      on kitchen appliances. But anyway, I didn't think the
      frogs

were very helpful. They wouldn't hold onto the raw yams,
      even when I cut them (the yams, that is!)
      into smaller chunks. The mashed yams were better;

the frogs made some pretty patterns as they hopped in the
      melted butter. I've attached another .jpeg
      showing that, but I know you won't think it's a
      poem.

As I'd expected, the frogs didn't really like it when I tried to
     write with them. They squirmed no end
     when I put their noses (or is it snouts?) to the page.

My roommate *did* say I could use her blender—for the last
     project, anyway. (Truthfully, she thinks your assignments
     are kinda intriguing.) But

I was looking at the cute little frogs hopping in the buttered
     yams, and I just *couldn't*. Sorry. I really
     do want a good grade in your course,

Professor, but maybe I'm just not cut out to be a poet? (I know
     we talked about MFA programs, but my daddy really
     wants me to go to law school, and I think

maybe he's right. I hope you understand.) My roommate
     wants you next semester, though, and she's a lot of fun.
     Have a great summer!

PS: I *was* glad we didn't have to "throw a crocodile in,"
     the way you said that your professor asked you to!

HAPPY FAMILY

Every day is celebration
yellow rosebud unknotting

granite shrugging its glitter
clouds in their chase

rain sloshing:

this happy balance,
this birthday.

FIREBLIGHT

They would talk about him in summer
—the grass parching, rhododendron shriveled,
flowers budding and blasted overnight, and
dry wind proposing in mudcakes
at the shrunken lake.

"Fireblight," a woman would say, old before her time.
Someone would nod and repeat it: "Fireblight"
spread down the line as we stood in the heat, waiting
for water, maybe ice beneath the sun.

The boy who took the rain. An old story in pieces.

A woman's life is a whole story, closewoven.
A boy's, a man's, it is fits and starts.

Everything growing he withered. Everything he loved
would die and crackle black around him. His grandmother
held him in a round garden, where he picked a sycamore leaf
arched large as his head. It crumpled and fled through his hand.

He touched the branch of an apple—it blackened and burned.

And the blight spread like fire in the orchard,
black branches, whole trees, black fruit falling,
leaves charring on the stem.

The boy loved his parents, but they aged and grew small
as he watched, dwindling.

His baby sister grew dark and thin; his brother grew fat and burst.

So the boy hid his fire in a lake that drained away.
He hid his fire in a stream that trickled to a halt.
He hid his fire in a wind that blew across the world

dragging the topsoil of seven dry and dying counties.

He hid his fire in a book, and the book just sang and sang,
and there the boy stayed, hearing the pages crackle and sing.

But books are never all there is, and the boy fell in love.

THE END OF THINGS

He wrote about her for years,
the way a felled tree oozes sap—

amber, topaz, crusted yellow—
through the wings of its wound,

through the small braceleted hands of its love

THE GIFT

Come.

Let this warm bundle of words

nuzzle under your arm,

and press each paw—

right there against your rib

—just long enough so that it hurts.

THE BOOK OF LOT

They all talk about my wife, the way
she turned back home: she said nothing.

Had she forgotten a book? To blow out a candle?
Had she only that hankering we all have, to see?

Is it a miracle I turned to drink?

Things in life there are that we shouldn't see,
I reckon. One of them is our homes dissolving into fire and brimstone

those times when the ashes fall, and a daughter says "Ain't that
a hand?" And you can only say "Hush" so much.

And one of them is your loved ones—just like that—turned dry crystal.

(Maybe she turned to talk to me? One hand tugging at a strap, her
lean body turning, the other brown hand rising as if to speak,

and the fingers going white, her face going ash,
her long hair blanching into tracery, her brown eyes
all a-shine, shining, shining. . .)

And one of them is your daughter's body rising above you in the dark,
her gentle body catching your seed. All of your shock, your rage, your guilt,

they come too late. You close your eyes, your body churning despite you.
Is it a miracle I turn to wine,

swinishly standing or sitting or struggling to sleep?

Now these infants nestle in their mothers' arms, and I—
I declare it a miracle, that thus—*thus* we are saved,
and I pour myself another long, dark drink.

Because of the weather (Happy Poem #2)

Because of the weather,
soft air brushing your cheek, your wrist,
and great gray cushions of cloud bundling

wonderfully down to the building-tops,
and the smells as rain-dark and ground-damp
as crouching in the wet garden in spring to find earthworms,
nightcrawlers, roly-polys—

("Sowbugs," my father called them, not knowing I would grow
to end a line, a poem—a happy poem—with such a childish name
as roly-poly.)

Sometimes we wake like
we change tires, bouncing hard
on an unbudging wrench.

HOW SLEEPING DOGS LIE

In dreams you run for miles without moving, your deft paws dragging then
as aimless and useless as puppies'. Waking you stare at me wide-eyed, a book
expressing tremendous unthinkable sentences
that might (but never do) illuminate.

Somewhere water drips from an untended faucet,
somewhere fresh markings stink and burn in love.

The Muse at Tsavo

The lioness lies beside me,
    her guard hairs prickling my skin,
        her body a vibration of the earth.

She is rank with sun, her belly
    taut with fresh gazelle,
        her smell a thick quilt of almost-pain

that sticks to the skin. I will never
    reach home. I will never know her.
        When she dreams I hear dark claws

extend, retract; the rasp of her
    tongue draws welts across skin,
        her tail the weight of spreading bruise.

The dusk wind freshens and takes
    her bundled violence from sleep.
        I hang on tight. I follow in her wake.

out my trailer door—
the mockingbird, the dew-wet
milk-crates full of light

On Being a Poet

On the days I am a poet,
I don't have to
write all the way to the end of the line:

On the days I am a poet,
I drive a '67 Volvo,
play the banjo, and have a happy dog.

On the days I am a poet
I can repeat myself.
I can repeat myself again,
and no one blinks.

I can repeat myself again,
but then people expect me to use new words
for the *schirrusch* the blanket makes
as it slides off a lover's body
on a cloudy morning,

or something crisp about gin.

On the days I am a poet
I can drink just enough.

On the days I am a poet
I have sex often,
not just muffled sex in the back seat of the Volvo,
but exotic nuzzling foreplay
on the black sand beach near Akrotiri,
or gasping toward climax in native azaleas
in the green light of our garden.

(My neighbor, Lord Byron, yells over to me
while he hacks at his crape myrtles: Jem, he says,
put more shagging in your poems—the girls'll eat that up.)

On the days I am a poet
I walk my happy dog around the lake.
Walt Whitman is walking his brown water dog,
his vague daughter feeding the short-winged coots.

On the days I am a poet
people believe everything I say.

On the days when I am a good poet
I believe it myself.

On the days when I am not so good,
I can still come home to my wife
and her *Hansestadt* pirate smile

saying Hilda and Sylvia are over for drinks
and something Byzantine,
and could I *pretty please* bring the gin.

The Volvo clicks as it cools in the garage,
the banjo repeats its scrap of sound,
and the happy dog plays in the yard.

Breakfast Gods & the Work of the Spirit

4.15, and coffee the only every god that I believe
for this five minutes, dripping like life by seconds
into our hot carafe. But yes, they coalesce: the caffeine,

the hard work, stiff muscles, raw eyes, even
the bright moon filtering down through empty dark.

Rabbit Watches

Who asked you? the garden asked.
We waited without answering, but
I privately thought that the garden had called,

holding up its shrivelled spinach arms,
chewed tentacles of mint,
torn, unnumbered leaves—

From here you smell the compost heap:
time's rot in this moonlit summer wind,
the garden's slow conquest, its sure and mineral revenge.

We breathe shallowly, watching for the dance the rabbits
make along the fenceline—slow, slow,
quickstep—and we finger our .22's.

No rabbits. Understanding why
one turns or doesn't in time, is that
in itself a perfection? I remember a taut rope

sliding in my hands, trying to decide on a value
to skin and blood as it slithered off.
Scar tissue's nerveless sometimes.

Stars fade in rain, wind pats us down,
I keep at arm's length both reason
and memory: No rabbits come down to the garden

no rabbits cross its dark straight lines, no mercy
needs to be shown. The chivalrous
rabbits mistrust the garden's quiet

and frustrate both our violence and love,
leave them to us like large-pawed things
that track the snow below windows, pausing to breathe

shallowly as they hear our clock-forced movements.
I clip out your name and wrap it
around your wet shoulders as we

leave the speaking garden
and the shipwrecked night
for the house and the kitchen's pardoning light.

THE DRAFT OF A POEM WITH TWO LINES

Your coracle cracks on this rough water.

TEACHING TANKAS

1.
Like pansies lifting
their faces to flashing sun
in unsteady wind,
student faces flash with thought,
ripple with their working minds.

2.
When you teach, someone
in the room is watching, each
part of each hour; goldfish-like
no plant can save you.
The eyes dissect, analyze
precisely: the way you've taught.

3.
Orange—the color
schoolbuses make before they
take you off to school—
How many syllables in orange?
In school? In each thin green seat?

Motive, Means, and Opportunity

As the mystery opens, we are late for the fondue party; we had to buy
    plates,
and milk, and isopropyl alcohol;

In the Icelandic crime tale, the boy's body lies in the crusted snow,
the elderly neighbor's dog following

maybe I glanced two seconds too long at the cover of *Vogue*? Maybe I
    pondered—70%?
91%?—too long in Pharmacy, where plastic bottles knock against each
    other.

a blood trail and small scrapes across hard ice from the playground; these
are letters the dog can read, slithered, scrabbled syntax. The dog

My son is nine; I picked him up on the way home, took him with me
into Kroger's lights, where everything is tidy, happier than long division,

tells the cold detectives how and where,
but won't say who, what motive generates, what pathways gathered

more kindly than afterschool mischance (cinnamon-sugar scattering on
    the floor),
brotherly deceit. His world has fallen, he has melted down.

or diverged in that broken frozen town. The forensic team arrives.
The wind intensifies. They collate, measure, seek the murder weapon; the
    cold detectives

The tears still glittered on his cheek as we searched among the pickles
and the baby oil, trying to remember where they keep the isopropyl
    alcohol.

gather statements, inform the grieving family, make early guesses bound
to be proved wrong in Chapter 3 or 9; the hunt moves

And now he disappears. We're late. I wait, plot thickening,
recalling a Safeway 40 years before, my father tracking me

on in bleak Icelandic landscapes, lava fields and falling snow, bitter wind;
the body count rises; the coldest detective sweats, fever burning

across six aisles: the motive, means, and opportunities of joy.
Candy I can dismiss; it isn't his first love. I glide

as he crawls a cheap acrylic carpet, dreaming of wind chill
and the boy's blood pooling on the ice. Regret tracks him close

the hardware aisle, rope and plungers,
hammers winking, slink through sundries—Post-Its

as his own losses, his broken family, the dark glass
where cold-blood murderer and colder detective meet

in neons or pastels, clever organizers, track his vibrant heart
beside the lobster tank. I find him, face and hands buried

merging and meshed, hunter hunted, chasing each
other across the thick-mossed lava and the glaciers

in the blue and yellow labels of the Hot Wheels carousel,
his eyes bright with the reds, jade greens, and indigos

solving any crime, any human way. You read it to its bitter, biting ending,
    and wonder
why we puzzle—we are always too late—over the dead instead of the living.

of tiny metal cars. "We're late," I say. He lifts a purple one
with real moving wings, unfolds his smile. He thinks that I'll say yes.

Resistance

I haven't the time to do what I want, much less grow this poem
you ask for; instead, like the crust that collects on a coral reef,

it dreams itself. As the wolf cuddles the deer in its zealous belly,
so this poem snows me in and under its scarred, triumphant bones.

IN YELLOW AND BLACK A FOUND POEM

Do not cross this line.

SMALL WONDER

A toddler
sweet as honey,
good as gold peaches,
tangerine as childish bliss,
lisped her nighttime prayers
beneath a small, stuffed, listening toy—
small wonder, as she grew,
year into year into year,
that she always knew
a god who was
androgynous
and plaid.

WORKSHOP

Sitka spruce, with its own thin clouds
of stitched silk:

Dark cola, clear glass, the reddening
apple leaning beside:

The poem slips like a squirrel
spiraling a trunk:

How human—
to want lessons in all.

A line — snow, sun, falling in together.

Epic Simile

I am like my mother.
You are like the sea.

When we sing together it is like wading in a tide pool still
  washed into
by fresh waves every now and then, hot and cold by turns,
  scaring the blue-shelled
crabs, our toes sinking and gripping, and you say *come
  back*
to look at this shiny shell this shadow this stone this
  curling wave these pelicans
creaking their wings above us.

When we walk up the beach with the children and the
  buckets and the rainbow
umbrella and the nylon cooler and the camera and the fat
  sandy books
it is not like singing, but like reading the famous poem
  where the sun is shining too
brightly sometimes and as each quatrain ends we reach
  another dune, more sea
oats, and the children drop to pick the stickle burrs out of
  their feet hopping and
mouncing, and we wait impatiently for the couplet.

Like my mother you carry the family forward singing into
  the dark cool pines.
Like the sea I come back and come back. And it shines.

Your rake rusts, vision
Spends itself. All build, all fail:
Let the wet leaves lie.

The gecko with her name across its tail

Maybe echoes of sky and willow
traced in eyes that move darkly,

maybe the milky
clouds that sweep the moon,

maybe your unlaced hair that
slips and weaves in a wind of silky
evening, a summer
lingering in storm-washed cities:

maybe these leave me
chastened in mind,
leave me the crushed
leaf of desire,

chilled lizard with his ditties
elegizing his lost loves,
by sun brushed.

CRAFT

Time and love make triangles,
    fish and fountains on the wall—
    but children make the butterflies
    and the dark, uneven rainbows that fumble when you call.

Time and love make moussaka,
    make stroganoff and tea—
    but children bring the peaches,
    bake the fish sticks, make the food you cannot see.

Time and love rent apartments
    build shelves and read their dreams—
    but children paint their yellow chairs
    and ride the red wheelbarrow home, bumping, shining.

Kudzu Harp

Let me play this kudzu harp
a while longer while the summer
is so green, and the poised
blue flowers that swell from each green string
sing out their noise

SIRENS

Like sirens in the night,
dead poems will stir you out of sleep,
and you stumble to the door in a fogbank
of dreamthought undone and there your
poem waits, saying—not for the first time—
I told you so. And so the sirens sing
the same sad song for us all, of
haunting fear—*have you done enough?*—
and confirmation —*you have done
so much!*—and over and over
they whisper in the shells of our
ears like the sea.

Fragile Things

I chisel a poem in glass
While somewhere a girl is crying

I tunnel sonnets through Styrofoam
As winter breaks and you wear green leaves

PARKING DECK

In the rain I watch the ghosts,
adjunct ghosts in chill disorder
just shy of Styx's serpentine;

it's ghosts that chisel into vision—
the small animals run down,
the deer who dying limps away

from a crumpled Ford, the
student who places her small frame
just before the charging Greyhound—

in the rain. They carve the bas relief
as if alive, or better, as if we too were ghosts,
threading our fox fire gowns in oilwash.

We speak so ill of living and of dead,
bracketed in chill disorder, suburban,
middle-aged, as wise as small owls:

meanwhile the ghosts—our living ghosts, our loved ones,
the death-pale kings and princes, too, all the dead
bitter beasts—work their chiseling,

they darken and make new this raining world.
I lock my car and turn into the chill disordered rain.

What people bring lunch
inside of says it all:
Bag or box, dream, grape.

Horn

1.
Down among the valves of your French horn, winking light or dark,
I have lived for forty years, my old boots a tattoo within your breath,

my morning commute along your fanfares locked in sound,
your small fingers pressing to shape a world which opens and closes,

which lengthens or collapses as your tongue ticks upward, as your lips kiss.

2.
Ever the darkness resounds with your body, despite my decrescendo,
your foot—on the chair in the nearly new studio—

taps time in vibrations that rise through your bones,
through your body on the cusp of its deep music, the horn

coming warm in your body and breath.

3.
One day the round world will vanish around us
in brass surprise, shivering in notes and partials;

one day your polished metal kiss
and your breath's belling tone

will have us vanish in a puff of sound.

4.
But I am drawn through you now like the past, where you stammered the lines
of a play we could never remember, the horn haunting or hunting

(and I never remember) after some suite by Telemann or Mahler,
but I remember your kiss shivering through the blonde lacquer,

I remember your soft hand in the bell of my world.

I dream you again
as the rose-bright thin-stemmed day.
This happens often.

the last haiku hears
your reading, feels your fingers
nibbling its blank coast

Book

You hold the book in your hand, slim, its glossy jacket
reflecting muted colors on your palm.

Slim, its weight a crescendo of maybes, partial tones
that slip on your hand like a baseball mitt the day

      your older brothers taught you how to catch.

THINKING OF LI PO WITH BANJO AT MOUNT CHEAHA

Four swarms of grackles chatter off,
One quiet cloud elopes:

This little mountain sings and grumbles,
staring at me as I stare back, thinking of Li Po,

sitting with an idle banjo.

Auroras: Carroll County, Illinois

Your ghost wears Wayfarers in English class,
dark shades like weak Boethian logic to watch the sun unsettling
on a horizon, unsettling, unwilling to admit
this sun almost only our dangerous eyes' creation
        (even to herself, even for herself).

Your transatlantic flight went down—the newspaper said it was ashes,
I thought it was ashes and funny twisted bits of quartz,
or what looked like quartz but it might have been glass.
"My mother," you said, "when I went home last time,
        had a poster of Elvis taped up in the laundry room,"

and you talked about desire, how it doesn't end
even when you don't want it any more, even after deaths and funerals,
and I thought how your Illinois flatlander ghosttalk
was like the red burst of cardinals lifting, exploding,
        in an unknown someone's backyard anywhere.

The heart shuffles backward and forward, running in place,
dodging the lazy rain. I'm drinking at Amy's Cafe with the beautiful dead,
and the heart shuffles backwards and forwards, the heart
—my heart—a fiction of agency, useful and useless by turns in our unquiet,
        this sadness, this invisible dark.

I want to tell you significant words, want to see you smile
in spite of your being dead, in spite of the things we've said, not said,
done or not done; instead I tell a tired old joke, twisting in the smoke of my
Merit cigarette, about how the examined life's not worth living either,
        and the heart shuffles back and forth across old banjo strings:

Agency forces this urgency, this engagement with fate,
acting as if we are free for a moment or two,
having or seeming to have,
like Nikolai killing the wolf in *War and Peace*,
   for an instant without thought, choice.

And whether you did or didn't, whether you fell or flew,
you, dead elegant, dead beautiful, remind me that you
could never do anything else, even if at the time it seemed really
as if there were agency, urgency, freedom of will.
   And yet the heart shuffles backwards and forth.

The Urgent County Roads, Driving the Cipher of You

Gravel fountains with travel;
the Gremlin hammers its shallow tattoo.

But I love the green light speed limit eyes of you—
    your scuppernong tequila skin—
    your Cinderella tiger teeth—
    the champagne Creole tongue
    of you and you and you.

HARD WORK

to say yes

HAPPY POEM #1

Eleven times this morning I have started to write this happy poem,
the poem that leaves the ink on your fingers,
the poem that leaves the perfect piece of crisp apple just to the very end,
the poem that exchanges your grief for a freshly laundered
handkerchief.

Eleven times this morning I have walked away afraid
to the other end of the desktop or the building or the beech trees out
    the window:
What do I know of happiness beyond words and love?
Beyond clicking keys or banjo strings?
Beyond fresh lawns and rough-tumbling animals?
Beyond hard work or your eyes when we meet by chance?
Beyond the roll of sea or the shape of a stone?
Beyond this crisp half-moment of perfection, or the next?

Eleven times I have tried to write this poem without thought, this poem
that will smile for you like the day when your child first walked,
this poem that will smooth in your hand like your first paycheck,
that will curl with achievement in your heart
like the memory of your first good kiss.

Eleven times I have walked away from this happy, happy poem.
And eleven times I have come back.

Too Small to Read (Reprise)

In your belly the poem grows,
Round as houses,
Big as hills,
Tall as tombs.

I tell you, "This is love,"
And in your belly the poem grows.